CW00347647

A Garden of Prayers

A Garden of Prayers

Reflections on the opening verses
to St John's Gospel

by Judith Leckie

Kevin
Mayhew

First published in Great Britain in 1995 by
KEVIN MAYHEW LTD
Rattlesden
Bury St Edmunds
Suffolk IP30 0SZ

ISBN 0 86209 641 3
Catalogue No 1440341

Printed in Hong Kong
by Colorcraft

FOREWORD

More than almost any other passage of scripture the prologue of St John's Gospel has been a source of comfort and hope to people everywhere. In a few words of great beauty it tells the whole story of God's love for humankind. It is the good news. It tells of sorrow, of hope, of great, great joy and love.

   My photographs which accompany these reflections were all taken in a monastery garden: a world in miniature. There are no sweeping vistas – rather creation is seen in a blossom, a blade of grass, the hands of the aged, a crucifix: the ordinary, the very ordinary things around us that we hardly ever 'see'.

JUDITH LECKIE

Sister Judith Leckie is a Carmelite nun at the Carmel of Our Lady of Walsingham, Langham, Norfolk.

In the beginning was the Word
and the Word was with God
and the Word was God...

As these tiny drops of dew
at the beginning of the day
reflect the dawn...

So much more does the Word Jesus
reflect for us the perfect image
of the Father.

All that is fresh and pure
and new is in him...

O LORD, HELP US ALWAYS TO SEE IN YOU
THE IMAGE OF OUR LOVING GOD.

*All things came into being
through him ...*

The grass withers,
the flower fades,
but the word of the Lord
lasts for ever ...

Perhaps we are afraid of fading,
of dying ...

But we and all created things
are held lovingly in the hands of God.

To *be* for all eternity.

O LORD, HELP US TO TRUST,
TO LIVE UNAFRAID.

Without him not one thing
came into being…

Human technology cannot create
such beauty as we see in this tiny ladybird.
Each loving detail is so perfectly
suited to its life.

Neither can human science create
a rejoicing heart.

True beauty is of God,
God alone is our rejoicing.

O LORD, WE THANK YOU
FOR THE GIFT OF BEAUTY.

What has come into being in him was life...

Coming into life isn't easy,
not for us,
not for any of creation...

There is struggle,
there is pain,
there is risk.

But there is also light and life
to draw us up – and out of the dark

to *become.*

O LORD, GIVE US COURAGE
AND THE WILL TRULY TO LIVE.

And the life was the light of all people...

Without light we could not see
the brilliance of these flowers...

Nor the beauty and texture of
their container.

Is it not the same when we look
at people?

We need the light of God in our hearts
to see the beauty of our neighbour.

O LORD, GIVE US YOUR LIGHT
SO THAT WE MAY ALWAYS SEE YOU IN OTHERS.

The light shines in the darkness...

Here is the play of light and shadow.

The darkness obscures,
the light reveals.

But we are often afraid of both of them.

We need not be, for the Light has come.

O LORD, HELP US TO WALK WITH CONFIDENCE,
FOR YOU ARE WITH US.

And the darkness did not overcome it ...

God's light,
God's peace,
God's love,

find their way through every
opening that we offer them ...

For God wills us to bring light
and life to others ...

God wills us to walk among the
fresh green trees of life.

O LORD, FILL US WITH YOUR PEACE,
YOUR LIGHT, YOUR SERENITY.

He was in the world...

The moment when this little
celandine blossomed with such radiance
was fleeting
like life itself.

The blossoming was a moment of pure gift:
joy for the heart,
light for the eyes...

Joy never lost but added to the sum of life.

A pale reflection of eternal joy.

O LORD, WE PRAY FOR THE GIFT OF JOY.

The world came into being through him . . .

Sometimes our own coming-into-being
feels like a journey through a stone wall . . .

searching for something,
someone,
to cling to.

Jesus offers himself to us as
our rock,
our safety,
our sure foundation.

O LORD, HELP US TO CLING TO YOU
IN ALL THE CIRCUMSTANCES OF OUR LIFE.

Yet the world did not know him...

Life is full of violence,
contradiction,
hurt.

We know it within ourselves
and in others.

We know too, that life comes even
out of death.

When we let the barbs in us be honed;
our knots be untied by love.

O LORD, HEAL THE HURTFULNESS
IN OUR HEARTS.

He came to what was his own
and his own people did not accept him…

Jesus is always offering himself
for our acceptance…

Many, many times we too reject him
in the lowly disguises of each day…

Each moment looks totally new
when seen
through his eyes
with his heart.

O LORD, GIVE US A HEART TO ACCEPT YOU.

To all who received him...
he gave power to become children of God...

There is great beauty
in old age if we would see it.

For it is the coming to fulfilment
of our lives.

The hands of the aged tell the
story of a lifetime of
work,
love,
suffering,
prayer...

O LORD, GIVE US THE GRACE
TO EMBRACE THE YEARS.

Who were born,
not of blood or of the will of the flesh
or of the will of man, but of God ...

To be born of the will of God
is to be offered Life and Light:

Life which carries us along the
uncertain path ahead ...

Light which leads us through
the shadows.

What will we choose?
Life with all its risk,
or death?

O LORD, WE NEED YOU TO BE OUR LIFE,
OUR LIGHT, OUR WAY.

The Word became flesh
and lived among us…

Walking on a clear frosty day
have you ever stopped
and looked?

Beauty is everywhere but we
must look…
must see…

And expect it in the ordinary.

O LORD, HELP US TO SEE YOU
IN THE ORDINARY

And we have seen his glory...

It is easy to see God's glory
in these beautiful flowers...

They fill our hearts with joy
and praise...

It is so much harder to see that same glory

in the oppressed,
in the poor,
in our neighbour,
in ourselves...

But it is there.

O LORD, MAY OUR EYES SEE YOU
IN ALL YOUR DISGUISES.

Full of grace and truth…

Purity,
Grace,
Truth.

These are to be cherished today.

We can ask for them,
pray for them,
live them…

O LORD, MAKE OUR HEARTS TRUTHFUL,
FILLED WITH YOUR GRACE.

From his fullness we have all received
grace upon grace…

The Word, Jesus, is the grace offered
– the bridge
between ourselves and God.

We find God by 'crossing'
that bridge…

It takes a lifetime to cross
but at the end is our eternal joy.

O LORD, HELP US TO RISK ALL
FOR LIFE IN ABUNDANCE.

Grace and truth came through Jesus Christ…

What is it about this little blackthorn blossom
that speaks of grace and truth?

It is so simple,
so straightforward…

It is what it is meant to be.

It is a tiny reflection of what is offered to us
in Jesus.

O LORD, HELP US TO BECOME
WHAT YOU WANT US TO BE.

No one has ever seen God…

When we look at a blade of grass
it does not look like this.

We do not see the light shining in
and through it as the camera does…

We also cannot see God,
except by light reflected
through the lens

of an open heart.

O LORD, OPEN OUR EYES TO
YOUR PRESENCE EVERYWHERE.

*It is the only son who is close to the
father's heart who has made him known ...*

What Jesus on the cross has shown us ...
is God's love.

Not a distant, uninvolved love,
but a love which is in the midst of
our suffering,
our pain ...

Is there, holding us,
knowing.

O LORD, WITH YOU WE ARE
NEVER ALONE, NEVER UNKNOWN.

ACKNOWLEDGEMENTS

We are grateful to the following for permission to reproduce photographs in this book:
Quidenham Cards, Carmelite Monastery, Quidenham, Norfolk for their permission to use the photographs on pps. 8, 10, 12, 22, 26, 30, 32, 34, 36, 38.
Carmel of Our Lady of Walsingham, Langham, Holt, Norfolk for photographs on pps. 6, 28, 40, 42.

The carving of a Station of the Cross on page 44 is by William Fairbanks, Bridgeham, Norfolk

Scripture quotations are from the Revised Standard Version of the Bible, copyright 1946, 1952, 1971 by the Division of Christian Education of the National Council of the Churches in the USA. Used by permission.